SAY YES TO COLLEGE...
SAY NO TO COLLEGE DEBT!

The Smart Family's Guide to Paying for College
without Losing your Savings, Sanity or Soul

By Nash Warfield

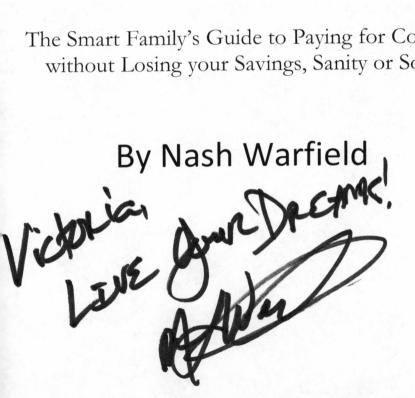

Victoria,
LIVE your DREAMS!

Dedication

This book is dedicated to the 3 most important women in my life:

Ja Nina Trinity Lee, my wife – Thank you for inspiring me to be a better man, accepting me as I am, and saving me from myself – I Love You to Infinity & Beyond...

BJ BrownLawson, my mother – Thank you for being my first teacher, for teaching AND showing me the value of hard work & perseverance – Your example is one that I will always strive to live up to...

Jett Lillian Lee Warfield, my daughter – Everything I do for the rest of my life is for you. My only job is to make you proud of me, and be the best possible example of fatherhood that I know how...

Contents

Part One: Say Yes To College............ 4

Part Two: Say No To College Dept! 26

Introduction: Why did I write this book?

G reetings! My name is Nash Warfield and before I start I want to personally thank you for purchasing this book. I truly appreciate the support and hope that you will get the return you are looking for. Now let me tell you why I wrote this book. I wrote this book because I am on a mission. I am on a mission to educate as many families of high school students as possible on the dangers of student loans. For the past 20 years I have traveled the country speaking to high school and college students about the importance of a college education, how to pick a major, and how to get in and succeed in college. I have seen many students empowered to make smart choices for their future by going to college and getting their education. However, I have also seen the dark side of the story. I have heard countless stories of students who have mired themselves in tens and sometimes hundreds of thousands of dollars in student loan debt. I have seen parents -- in the name of trying to "help" their child pay for college -- put themselves in a huge financial hole with parent loans, crippling their chances for a productive retirement. I have witnessed the stress that it puts on the relationship between parent and child when the child doesn't pay back loans the parent co-signed. There are so many disadvantages and negative outcomes from college debt that far outweigh any possible benefit.

However, college debt has become the norm in the United States. There is a pervasive belief in this culture that it is impossible to go to college without debt. Many people have assumed the victim mentality that in order to go to college today, they have to take on tens of thousands of dollars in student loans and parent loans. The purpose of this book is to counteract that belief. My goal is to show you that going to college debt-free is ABSOLUTELY POSSIBLE and is accomplished every year by thousands of families. It all comes down to two words: MINDSET and CHOICES. This book will teach you the proper mindset you need towards paying for college, and how to make the right choices when it comes to selecting and paying for college. Let me warn you: Much of what you will read here is the complete OPPOSITE of what is taught in our culture today. These are ideas that go against the norm of what most people say about paying for college. However, normal in the country is a miserable college graduate with $50,000 of student loans tied around their ankle like a ball and chain. On the cover of the book you see the image of that chain being cut. That is my goal -- to break the chains of college debt in this country. To break the cycle of normal and miserable. It will not be easy. It will require some difficult choices, some tough conversations, and may not make you parents very popular with your children. But I am not trying to make parents more popular. I am trying to save your retirement, help you keep your sanity and keep from losing your soul in the name of trying to pay for college for your child. I am trying to help you understand that while graduating from college is extremely important, it can be done the right way - - and the right way is DEBT-FREE. When you have finished this book, I want you to know beyond a shadow of a doubt that you can...

SAY YES TO COLLEGE... SAY NO COLLEGE DEBT!

How You Should Read This Book

This book is separated into two sections. The first section "Say YES to College" focuses on the benefits of going to college, how to choose the right college for you, and how to get into the college of your choice. The second section "Say NO to College Debt" focuses on how to pay college without student loans or parent loans. You don't have to read the book from beginning to end – you can choose what section you want to read first based on what's more important to you. The format is primarily Q&A – answers to the most important questions I've received and researched about college over the past 20 years of speaking to high school students and parents. Rather than a book, you can use this as more of a resource guide that can be picked up whenever you have a specific question that you would like answered. My hope is that you will come back to this book over and over again as you go through your college planning process. I want to give you the confidence to know that YES – you can go to and graduate from college today WITHOUT debt and I firmly believe that this book will help you accomplish that goal.

PART ONE

SAY YES TO COLLEGE

Is a college degree still necessary?

In my presentations to high school students, one of the most common questions I get is: "Nash, do I still need to go to college? Is a college degree even still necessary to succeed in today's world?" There has been a lot of talk in the media recently that you no longer need a college degree to make it in today's society. I think nothing could be further from the truth. While a college degree may not be absolutely necessary, some type of post-secondary education AFTER high school is critical to your success. Obviously it depends on your choice of career field that you want to enter. For example, if your dream is to work on cars and be an auto mechanic, you wouldn't need a college degree, but a trade school would definitely be in your future. If you wanted to go into graphic design or computer programming, the tech world is changing so rapidly by the time you get a 4-year degree the information you learned would be outdated. In this case a 2-year degree or a specialized certification in the program you want to learn would be the best route. However, if you want go into some of the more traditional careers (teacher, lawyer, doctor, accountant, etc.), then you ABSOLUTELY need at least a 4 year degree to have access to those fields.

How much money will I make with a college degree?

While there are no guarantees, according to 2018 data from the U.S. Bureau of Labor, here are the average salaries you can expect based on your level of education:

High School Graduate:	$35,256
Associates (2 year) Degree:	$41,496
Bachelors (4 year) Degree:	$59,124
Masters Degree:	$69,732
Doctorate (PhD) Degree:	$84,396
Professional (MD, JD) Degree:	$89,960

As I said these are averages. There are high school dropouts who are multimillionaires, and there are doctors who make $50,000 per year, but as you can see you will make more money with a college degree overall than if you don't have one. So I say again, if you want to make more money, SAY YES TO COLLEGE!

How much does it cost to live in society today?

epending on where you live in the country, these numbers will vary. Obviously it costs more to live in Manhattan, New York than in Manhattan, Kansas but here are the average amounts you can expect to pay when you get out in the "real world"

Rent:	$1100
Electric/Heat:	$100
Water:	$50
Cable/Internet:	$150
Cell Phone:	$100
Car Payment:	$350
Insurance:	$200
Gas:	$300
Maintenance:	$75
Groceries:	$150
Entertainment:	$150
Misc:	$100
Savings:	$100
Total Monthly Expenses:	$2875
Total Annual Expenses:	$2875 X 12 =$34,500

There are several items I left off – clothes, travel, etc. – since I'm just looking at basic minimum expenses needed to live a decent life in America today. So this means that AFTER TAXES (since Uncle Sam has to get his share), you need to bring home at least $2875 per month or $34,500 per year to live an average decent life today.

Now let's assume you skip the college option and decide to get a full-time job working 40 hours per week after finishing high school. Let's say that job pays you $10 per hour. And let's further assume that you take NO vacation and work 52 weeks per year. So here is what you will earn:

40 hours/week X $10/hour X 52 weeks/year = $20,800

And that is BEFORE TAXES!!! Can you see the problem? Working a full-time job after high school and not getting more education very likely will NOT allow you to make the kind of money you need to live an average decent life in America today. You will be living with your parents in their basement for the rest of your life! So again I say – **SAY YES TO COLLEGE!!!**

What are advantages & disadvantages of a 4 year college?

Advantages:

Highest **Earning Power:** The average person with a 4 year degree will over a lifetime earn more than a million dollars *above* what someone with a high school diploma will earn. The average person with a 2 year degree will earn $500,000 more than a person with a high school diploma. So if you want to make more money, get a degree!

Get Away from Home: For those of you who want to get as far away from your parents as possible (go on, admit it), going to a 4 year college gives you the opportunity to go to any state in the country -- or almost any country in the world -- to get your degree.

Big-Time Sports Programs: Do you want access to Duke University basketball or Michigan football games? College puts you in the environment to be around the biggest sports programs in the country, and even if you don't go to the biggest schools, the sports life at most colleges is one that many students enjoy as a way to socialize and foster school spirit.

Social Life: Want to join a fraternity or sorority? Looking for clubs to meet like-minded individuals? College is one of the best ways to create lifelong friendships and relationships. You never know, you just may meet your future spouse in college. (I did!)

Disadvantages:

Highest Cost: I imagine you're reading this book because you're concerned about the cost of college. Obviously the range of cost varies for 4 year colleges, depending on where you go, but some of you who are looking at Ivy League or other "elite" colleges can spend up to $60,000 per year *for tuition alone!* I will delve further into college costs in Part 2: Say NO to College Debt.

Student Loan Debt: Again, I imagine you're reading this book because you want to avoid college debt. Part 2 of this book focuses on how to go to college without student loans or parent loans which have had devastating effects on millions of young people and families in this country. If you want to skip straight to that section, feel free to do so.

50% Graduation Rate: Did you know only half of students who go to 4 year colleges graduate? Definitely consider this as you make your college decision. If you plan to start, plan to FINISH!

6.5 Years to Graduate: Did you know it takes the average student 6.5 years to graduate from a 4 year college? So if you spend more time in college, what are you also spending more of? That's right – MONEY! So if you go a 4 year college, make it your goal to finish in 4 YEARS!

(Source: Chronicle of Higher Education - 2013 College Completion Report)

What are the advantages & disadvantages of going to a community college?

Advantages:

Less expensive for basic courses: No matter which college you choose to attend, your first year and a half you will take for the most part the EXACT same courses: Math, English, History, etc. They are part of the General Education requirements. You can go a 2-year college and take these courses for A LOT less money than they cost at a 4 year college. So if you're looking for the least expensive way to get a degree, a 2 year community college may be the right choice for you.

Higher earning power: The average person with a 2-year degree will earn $500,000 more over their lifetime than a person with a high school diploma – so simply going to community college puts you in a better position to make more money than not going to college at all.

Transfer to 4 year college: After getting your 2 year degree – also called an associate's degree – you can take those credits and transfer them to just about any 4 year college you choose to get your bachelor's degree. I have been working with employers and hiring managers for the last 20 years, and they DO NOT CARE if you got an associate's degree from one school and a bachelor's degree from another. If you have the skills, you WILL get hired.

Close to home: Some of you don't want to go far away from home for college. You like eating Mom's home-cooked meals and sleeping in your own bed every night. Well, that's your only choice because the majority of 2 year colleges do not offer on-campus housing, so if you like living at home, this can be the way to go. FYI: This is another way to save THOUSANDS in housing costs for college as well. Housing costs at 4 year colleges average between $12,000 and 15,000 per year, so commuting from home can save you as much as $60,000.

Disadvantages:

Negative Perception: Whether it's true or not, there is a negative perception that community colleges have. Some people believe the education is not as quality as 4 year colleges, and the only people that go to community colleges are people who couldn't get in to 4 year colleges. I will tell you with 1000% certainty that NOTHING is further from the truth. Community colleges offer excellent education, and there are many very successful people who started at community college – but either way the perception still exists.

"13th Grade": This is a negative nickname that community college is sometimes called. Because many of your high school classmates choose to go to the local community college, some people feel that it is just an extension of high school. Again, it's just a perception, but it is one to consider when making your choice.

Live at home: Some of you DO NOT like your mother's home cooking. Some of you DO NOT like sleeping in your own bed. As I mentioned you don't have a choice when you go to a 2 year college because most do not offer a housing option, so you will most likely be commuting from home.

More education needed: If you want to be a teacher, an accountant or an engineer, obviously you will need more education than just an associate's degree to achieve that goal. You will need at least bachelor's or in some cases a master's degree to obtain those jobs.

Average 3.2 years to graduate: It takes the average person 3.2 years to graduate from a 2 year college. Again, you want to consider this when making your final college choice.

What are the advantages & disadvantages of a career school/technical school?

Advantages:

Specific Education: If you want to go into a specific career field, like auto repair, HVAC or cosmetology, a career or technical college is the best route for you. At a technical college, you only take classes geared toward one specific career, as opposed to traditional colleges where you take a wide range of general education classes not focused on a particular career path. This saves you both time and money because you're not paying for and attending classes you don't necessarily need.

Shorter Program Length: Most technical schools can be completed in less than 2 years. Technical colleges also start class more frequently than other schools, saving you time because you don't have to wait for the fall semester to start. Most technical colleges also go year-round rather than having the long winter and summer breaks at other colleges. What this means to you is you get into your career quicker – a great option if that's what you're looking for.

Career-focused education: This means that when you graduate from the college you should have the skills and experience needed to succeed in your field. They also provide a learning environment very similar to a workplace setting. Most tech schools provide hands-on learning and have instructors who are highly skilled, experienced and connected in the fields they teach. Technical colleges also provide career-service advisors to assist students in searching for a job after graduation.

Disadvantages:

For-Profit Colleges: Technical colleges are also called for-profit colleges, which have gotten a bad reputation in recent years for admissions practices, misleading job-placement statistics, and higher student-loan default rates. Make sure you do thorough research on the college you are choosing, as you should with any college.

High Cost: Even though the program length is shorter, technical colleges can still be very pricey. Just like 4 year colleges, you need to consider the cost when choosing this option.

Transferring Credits: If you want to take your credits to another school, it is usually more difficult to transfer credits from a technical college to a traditional 4 year school. This is another important consideration when making your final college choice.

What should I look for in a college?

Now that you know what types of colleges you can choose from, here are the factors you should look at when choosing from the nearly 5,000 colleges in the United States today.

PRICE: We will get more into this in the section on paying for college, but obviously the #1 factor in determining where you go to college is IF YOU CAN YOU AFFORD IT. Do not automatically rule out schools based on price, but your final choice should absolutely depend on if you are able to write the check for 4 years WITH NO DEBT. You also want to consider financial assistance from the school as over 65% students do receive some financial aid from colleges.

College Size: Do you want to go to a school with 4,000 students or 40,000 students? The number of students will impact class size and student-teacher ratios. Will you feel comfortable in a class of 300 students in a large auditorium, or do you need more personalized attention from your professor? Every student is different, so knowing what environment is right for you and where you will be successful is critical when determining where you decide to attend.

Strength in your major: Not only should you make sure the college offers your major, make sure it has strong program in that major. And just because it's a bigger or a "well known" school doesn't mean that the program is better.

Competitiveness of school: Some schools are really tough to get admitted to, and some are less competitive. You'll want to apply to both kinds of schools to keep your options open.

Opportunities outside the classroom: College is not all classroom education; you also want to make sure you're getting a well-rounded experience. Are there certain clubs or extracurricular activities you want to join? Do you like to ski or surf? Does the college offer study-abroad programs? Make sure you consider your college experience – both inside and outside the classroom.

How do colleges make their admissions decisions?

There are 8 factors that colleges use to make their admissions decisions. If you think of the word **C-R-I-T-E-R-I-A**, it's an easy way to remember all 8 factors:

Course Selection: Colleges will look at the courses you've taken in high school to determine admission. Usually the tougher the courses you take and do well in, the better your chances for admission. You may consider taking Advanced Placement (AP) courses to improve your odds.

Rank: Colleges want to know how well you match up against your classmates, so class rank is another factor for admissions. If your school doesn't do class ranking, they should offer a School Profile which shows how they compare to other schools. Talk to your guidance counselor about this.

Interests: Colleges want well-rounded students, not just the student with the 4.0 GPA. Your activities outside the classroom matter as well, so whether you play sports, join the band or compete on the debate team, it's important that you're not only a member of those clubs, but also show involvement as well. Seek to make a difference in the clubs you join.

Test Scores: It goes without saying that your SAT and ACT scores are huge factors in admissions decisions at most colleges, so you want to do as well on these tests as possible. Find out from your college of interest which test they require, because different colleges look at different tests. Test scores are also a criteria for college scholarships, so it is well worth the investment to take a test-prep course to help improve your scores as much as possible. Lastly, take the tests more than once, as colleges look at your best performance on each test, and the more often you take them, the higher you scores can get.

Essays: Your personal story is what will separate you from the thousands of applicants that admissions officers will review, so make your story a good one. It's not important to impress them with big, fancy words; it's more important to highlight what makes you different from everyone else and what kind of impact you will make on that school. And it's critical to both spell-check and proofread your essay – you don't want to make a bad impression with misspelled words and poor grammar. It's a good idea to have your English teacher review your essay before submitting.

Recommendations: You want letters from teachers who really know you, not just ones who gave you an A in their class. You want community leaders, sports coaches or employers to talk about who you are and what type of difference you will make on the campus. And please be courteous to your teachers and counselors and give them PLENTY of time to write these letters. Nothing frustrates teachers more than seniors who come to them at the last minute to write a letter, along with the 30 other last-minute requests made by other students. If you want a quality letter, give plenty of notice.

Interviews: Some colleges require interviews for admission, some do not. Find out from the college if an interview is required. And if it is optional, you DEFINITELY want to go on an interview. Once again, it gives the college a chance to get to know you personally and put a face with the application. It's another way to stand out from the many other applicants they will consider.

Academic Performance: Most colleges will look at your grades as their primary factor for admissions consideration. Some of the more competitive colleges will start at GPA and throw away any application below a 3.0 – there are just too many to look through and they narrow their search pretty quickly. So you obviously want to get the highest grades possible to get into the college of your choice. A word of caution: Don't slack off spring semester of your senior year, as some colleges will ask you to submit those grades even after you've been accepted. So don't let "senioritis" keep you from getting into your dream school.

Source: Making It Count Programs

What admissions terms should I be familiar with?

Acceptance: The decision by an admissions officer or committee to offer the opportunity for enrollment as a student at a particular institution.

Deferred Admission: A category of admission used in conjunction with early applicants to indicate that a student has not been admitted early but will remain in the applicant pool for reconsideration during the review of applications for regular admissions.

Deferred Enrollment: This is a category of admission available at some institutions for fully accepted students who wish—for a justifiable reason—to take a semester or year off before enrolling in college.

Denial: The decision by an admissions officer or committee not to offer an opportunity for enrollment.

Early Action: When a prospective student applies for admission by early deadline (before the regular admission deadline) and receives notice of acceptance, denial or deferment with no obligation to the university to enroll, if accepted for admission.

Early Admission: Through this program, qualifying high school juniors with outstanding academic records may forgo their senior year in high school and enroll in a college or university.

Early Decision: Through this program offered by many post-secondary schools, students willing to commit to a school if accepted submit their application by a date well before the general admission deadline. If accepted, the student must enroll in that school, so students should only apply in this manner to their first-choice school.

Notification Date: The date by which applicants who are accepted for admission are expected to notify the institutions of their intent to enroll and make enrollment deposits. This date is usually on or around May 1st.

Rolling Admissions: This is a practice used by some institutions to review and complete applications as they arrive, rather than according to a set deadline.

Waitlist: An applicant is put on the waitlist when an admissions officer or committee decides to offer the applicant the opportunity to enroll in the institution only if there is space available in the incoming class after fully admitted students have responded to their offers to enroll. This category of admissions is reserved for students whose profiles are strong, but who are marginally qualified in comparison to the overall strength of others in the pool of applicants.

Source: www.firstinthefamily.org

How many colleges should I apply to? When should I submit my applications?

It is a good idea to apply to a variety of colleges. Even if you have had your heart set on one college since you were 5 years old, you still want to give yourself options for your decision. Here are some thing you want to consider:

Highly selective or less selective?: You want to apply to some tough schools to get into, as well as some that aren't so tough. The more options, the better.

Close to home or far from home?: When I speak to high school juniors, I ask them how many want to go far from home for college. About 90% of the audience will raise their hand. When I ask that same question to high school seniors, less than half raise their hand. The closer students get to graduation, the less inclined they are to leaving the comforts of their home state for college. So you'll want to apply to both types of schools -- again, to give yourself options.

Applying to anywhere from 5 to 7 colleges across the spectrum just discussed -- is a good benchmark. In terms of when to apply, I advise students to have all applications completed by Christmas vacation of your senior year. Think of it as a Christmas present to yourself, one that allows you to relax over the break and enjoy the time with your family. It also frees you up to spend the spring semester focused on scholarship applications, which we will talk more about in Section 2 in paying for college.

What should I do on a college visit?

Talk to 'real students': Not just your tour guide, whose job is to tell you everything great about the school and why you should go there. You also want the perspective of regular students, so be willing to approach a couple of them on campus and ask about their experiences at the college. You're far more likely to get a more unbiased perspective.

Visit a classroom: Ideally while an a class is in session. You'll get a feel for the learning environment and a sense of how comfortable you'll feel in larger (or smaller) classes. You will also gain perspective on the teaching style of an actual college professor.

Meet a professor: If you can, talk with a professor who teaches a class in the major that interests you. You can get further insight as to what the major involves and what it takes to be successful. They may also be able to give you ideas on possible career tracks for that major.

Interview with an admissions officer: If a college interview is optional, you definitely want to opt for the interview. Again, they get to associate a name with a face and not just a random application. If you plan on playing sports, also aim for some face-to-face time with a coach of your prospective sport.

Ask tough questions: Keep in mind that YOU are the customer and that colleges compete for your business. So ask questions to make sure the college is a good fit for you. Examples include: What % of students graduate? What is the job placement % for students in my major? What % of students get into the graduate school of their choice? (if grad school is in your future)

Visit the Career Center: Remember the primary goal of college is to get a quality job in your major. At the Career Center, you can find out what companies recruit at the college, check out internship opportunities (critical), and find out common first jobs for students in your major.

Visit Other Places of Interest: Check out the places where you will be spending much of your time. The library, fitness center, dining hall, bookstore and freshman dorms are most likely stops you'll want to make.

How should I pick a major? Why is it important to pick the right major for me?

Did you know that 85% of Americans hate their job? That's right, 85% of people go to work every day mad because they hate what they do for a living. Some of you know your parents hate their job. You see them come home from work mad every day. They come home from work -- and kick the cat -- because they are mad. You don't want to be this person 20 years from now. You want to enjoy what you do for a living. After all, you will be doing it for the next 40 years of your life. And I think the reason so many people hate their job is so many students choose the WRONG major for the WRONG reasons -- so they end up in the WRONG career for them and wind up kicking cats. This is why it is critical to choose the right major for you.

But what is the right major for you? How do you pick a major? There are two words you want to think about when choosing your major: STRENGTHS and INTERESTS. What is a strength? A strength is something you are good at. What are you naturally good at? What topics come easy to you? What subjects in school do you easily excel at? Is it Math? Science? Writing? Art? Think of your strengths as a starting point.

The next word to consider is INTERESTS. What is an interest? An interest is something you like to do. What topics do you enjoy talking about? What subjects really get you excited? If I gave you two minutes to talk on any subject matter what would it be? Is it sports? Music? Fashion? Travel? What topics really mean a lot to you and get your blood flowing?

Now here is how you choose your major: COMBINE YOUR STRENGTHS & INTERESTS. What does that mean? Here are a few examples. Let's say you're really good at math, but you like sports. Maybe you become an accountant for a professional sports team. How about if you're good at writing and you love talking about music? Perhaps you become a music journalist. If computing is a strength and video games are your love, you could be looking at video-game design as a career. These are just a few examples to show that when you combine your strengths and interests, you have a solid chance of identifying the major -- and career -- that's right for you. And you won't end up kicking cats when you're 40 years old.

What other factors should I consider when choosing a major?

In addition to strengths and interests, the third factor you want to think about when choosing your major is the future job market. According to the Department of Labor, here are the 4 hottest fields for job opportunities during the next 10 years:

Health Care (particularly Nursing): The population is aging, and the Baby Boomer generation will have rising health care needs. Because of that, there will be many jobs in the health care field, especially if you're looking to major in nursing. There is already of shortage of nurses, and there are many positions that will need to be filled.

Business (particularly Accounting): Everything is a business -- from your iPhone to your Air Jordans to this book you're reading now. Business makes the world go 'round, and there will always be jobs for those looking to enter the business world. Even though successful businessmen are often portrayed in media as evil, greedy capitalist pigs who want to destroy the world, nothing is further from the truth. Business people are actually among the most philanthropic, service-oriented people on the planet and there is absolutely nothing wrong with being associated with it. Accounting is a particular field that has lots of upside, as business will always need people who are good with numbers.

Technology (particularly Computers): It goes without saying that technology is changing constantly, and those who keep up with it will be at the forefront of the job market. There will be millions of jobs in the tech world, involving everything from apps to social media to hardware and software. Computers aren't going anywhere, and if you're good with computers, it's a great field to find a job.

Education: Millions of teachers are retiring across the country, and those positions need to be filled. There is a major need to educate our future leaders and labor force, and if you enjoy working with young people, there will be a job for you in the classroom.

These are the 4 hottest job markets for the near future. Am I saying that all of you reading this book should major in one of these fields? Of course not. But you absolutely should find out what kind of jobs there will be in your potential major. I have seen some rather ridiculous majors that students choose, with very little market value or job potential. Don't major in underwater basket-weaving or left-handed puppetry, because there are NO JOBS in those fields. Of course I'm being extreme, but please consider the job potential for the major you choose. The only thing worse than having a degree with debt, is a useless degree with debt and no job.

OK - now that we have thoroughly discussed why you should go to college and how to get in, let's get into why I know you REALLY picked up this book - **HOW TO TO GO COLLEGE WITH NO DEBT!**

SAY NO TO COLLEGE DEBT

How much student loan debt is there in America? What is the primary cause?

There is a student loan crisis in this country. According to the Federal Reserve Bank of New York in 2018 there is currently over 1.5 TRILLION DOLLARS in student loan debt. That's TRILLION with a T-R; that's over 1,500 BILLION! It's the largest personal debt in America -- more than both credit cards ($931 billion) and car loans ($1.22 trillion).

In my opinion, the biggest reason there is $1.5 trillion in student loan debt is POOR COLLEGE CHOICES. Millions of students are making HORRIBLE choices about where they go to college, and it is causing them to go into massive unnecessary debt. Over the past 20 years of speaking to high school and college students, I have seen the same scenario repeatedly:

A student gets all hyped up over certain college they want to go to -- perhaps because of a high-profile sports program or a particularly stunning campus.

The school costs $50,000/year in tuition and the family only has $10,000 they can pay.

The student takes out $40,000/year in student loans for a total of $160,000.

The student majors in underwater firefighting or something ridiculous and they're paying back student loans until they're 50!

This is a BAD PLAN -- DON'T DO THIS! You have to be smart about how you choose your college. For some reason, in this country we've become DUMB about education (how oxy*moronic*, right?). Here is the best way to avoid college debt: GO TO A COLLEGE YOU CAN AFFORD! Just like you wouldn't go to a car dealership and buy a $100,000 car you can't afford, DO NOT GO TO A $100,000 COLLEGE YOU CANNOT AFFORD. Going into student loan debt is one of the WORST decisions you can make, and you will regret it for years to come. I am hoping and praying this book will steer you away from that terrible mistake.

Why is college tuition so high? Why does it continue to rise?

One of the most frustrating and scary things for families about college is looking at the sticker price. You have some colleges like Vanderbilt University in Nashville, Tennessee, that cost over $62,000/year to attend. You'd be looking at a quarter million dollars for a 4 year education! Not making any judgements on Vanderbilt, but you may be asking why is the cost of college so high? And why does it seem to go up every year?

The main reason college costs so much is the federal student loan program. Most people don't realize that most student loans are federally insured. I'm not talking private student loans from a bank. These are the loans you apply for through the FAFSA form we will discuss later. So here's what happened: At some point some some "genius" senators in our government got together and thought it would a be a good idea to give 18-year-olds unlimited unsecured loans. No job history, no prospects on how they were going to repay it -- just give them the loans because education is "so important." If any banker in America made these kind of loans, they would be fired immediately. But our leaders in government (on both sides of the political aisle, by the way) thought this was a good idea. And here's the kicker: If the student defaults on the loan and can't pay it back, THE GOVERNMENT PAYS THE MONEY TO THE COLLEGE! And by government, who does that mean? That's right: you and me, the TAXPAYERS! So we get to pay back the loans to the college that the 18-year-olds should have never taken in the first place and now can't pay.

So understand that colleges have NO incentive to lower tuition costs. They know that they are getting their money regardless because of the federally insured student loan program! And that is why college tuition will continue to rise. And as long as students can borrow $250,000 to go to schools like Vanderbilt and we the taxpayers are backing it up, college tuition will continue to skyrocket now and into the future. It is a BROKEN program that must stop. There's just no way it can sustain itself!

What mentality should you have towards paying for college?

Before there were cars, people traveled on horse and buggy. Before there were cell phones, people communicated on pay phones and landlines. And they got along just fine. You may be thinking, "Nash, where are you going with this?" Here is the BEST way to think about paying for college: What if student loans and parent loans didn't exist? What if there was NO WAY to borrow money for a college education? How would you pay for college then? Easy -- you would choose the college your family can afford based on your ACTUAL budget. So I want you to pretend that there are NO SUCH THING as student loans and parent loans. Act as if the ONLY way you can pay for college is by paying out of your pocket. That will dramatically change the way you go about looking at colleges -- and definitely for the better. Then you will determine a college based on actual value and return on investment, not relying on massive loan debt to get you through your education.

Is this a radical way to think about paying for college? Maybe. But as the saying goes, drastic times call for drastic measures. If we are ever going to tackle this student loan crisis, it will take radical measures by families to make smarter choices about where you send your child to college. Just as it's unwise to go $100,000 in debt for a luxury car that you can't afford, the same principle applies here: Do NOT permit yourself or your child to take on $50K, $70K or $100K of debt for an education that your family cannot afford. IT IS SIMPLY NOT WORTH IT.

So act like college debt doesn't exist. Take debt off the table. When you start with that mindset, it can ease much of the stress and pressure parents feel about paying for college.

What are the consequences of student loans?

While the obvious downside of student loans is years of repaying debt, there are other consequences that come along with it. The primary consequence of high student loan debt is it limits your choices. In life you want to be free to make as many choices as possible, and the irony is that choosing to take out student loans severely limits your choices. Here are some examples that I've seen over the years:

–   The 27-year-old new mom who wants to quit work and stay at home with her baby, but she can't because she has $75,000 in student loans

–   The 24-year-old guy who is called to do mission work, but he can't take the opportunity because he has $90,000 in student loans

–   The 25-year-old graduate who has to stay in a job he hates because he has over $100,000 in student loans to repay

–   The 65-year-old parent who wants to retire from the workforce but can't because they have committed to $90,000 of parent loans for their child's education

–   A higher percentage of people in their 20s living at home with parents longer because they can't afford to live on their own because of their student loan payments

–   A higher percentage of people in their 20s waiting longer to get married because of their student loans

–   A higher percentage of people are waiting longer to have children because of their student loans

–   Home ownership is at its lowest rate in 50 years (Source: U.S. Census Bureau) because people can't afford to buy homes because of their student loans

- Higher rates of depression and even suicide are showing up among people in their 20s on account of massive student debt loads (Source: CDC)

These are the consequences that students and families don't think about when going into debt for college. You have to think LONG-TERM about the choices you make when it comes to paying for college. And while college loans may seem like a good short-term solution, you can clearly see they have painful long-term consequences. Whether you're the parent or the student, don't let college debt limit your choices for the next 30 years of your life.

What is the value of an in-state public school vs. a private school?

L et's compare two colleges. I live in New Jersey so for this example I will choose two colleges based here. Let's consider a bachelor's degree in business from Kean University, a state-run college in Union, and the same degree from Rider University, a private college in Trenton. For the fall of 2018, annual tuition at Kean University will cost you about $12,000 -- yielding a 4-year total of $48,000. To get the EXACT SAME degree from Rider University, the 4-year cost is $168,000 ($42,000 per year). With all due respect to the folks at Rider, one has to ask: Can the Rider degree really be almost 4 TIMES BETTER than the Kean degree? Does anyone SERIOUSLY think the Rider degree will help someone earn almost 4 TIMES as much money as the Kean degree can? This is what many families fail to consider when it comes to college choice: RETURN ON INVESTMENT. The point of college is to get a job in your chosen field, and if a $48,000 degree will do that nearly as well as a $168,000 degree, then why pay $120,000 more for the EXACT same outcome? And for sure, why take on $120,000 in additional debt for the same outcome? This is the kind of poor analysis and decision-making that has led to $1.5 trillion dollars in student loan debt, and this is exactly what needs to change if we are ever to have any chance of solving this crisis. Families, I beg you: THINK BEFORE YOU SPEND! Ask yourself: Is spending 4 times as much on a private college vs. an in-state public school worth the investment? In 99.9% of the cases, the answer is a resounding NO!

Sidebar: You can do this same comparison for schools in any state. Here are a few more examples listing annual TUITION ONLY for Fall 2018:

University of Maryland - $10,495 vs.

Loyola University (MD) - $48,718

Georgia State University - $10,858 vs.

Emory University (GA) - $46,314

University of Tennessee - $12,970 vs.

Vanderbilt University (TN) - $48,600

Will I make more money attending a private school or a big-name school?

The biggest myth about college in our society today is that you will be more successful based on the college that you attend. NOTHING could be further from the truth. In fact, there is ZERO CORRELATION between the school you go to and how much money you will make in life. Princeton University did a recent study where they compared the average starting salaries of people who graduated from Ivy League colleges against people who got ACCEPTED to Ivy League colleges and then decided to attend a lesser-known institution. You know what they found? There was NO difference! What does this mean? It means successful people come from everywhere and the name on your degree DOES NOT mean anything when it comes to salary or success. Another study found that 80% of CEOs of Fortune 500 companies (who are in the top .05% of salaries in the US) attended in-state public colleges! (Source: US News & World Report)

So PLEASE do not believe the hype that you will be more successful or make more money by going to a private university vs an in-state public university. There is simply no research or data anywhere to back up that notion. For 99% of the jobs in this country, the name on the degree means NOTHING. What matters is the grades you got, the impact you made in groups you joined, and the relationships you built with professors and advisers. Showing you can get the job done is infinitely more important than the school you graduated from. And it certainly makes ZERO sense to go into debt for an education that simply doesn't give you any advantage in the job market. This goes back to my last point on ROI (return on investment). DO NOT GO INTO DEBT FOR YOUR EDUCATION; IT IS NOT WORTH IT! (Have I said that enough times yet?)

What causes student loans more than any other factor?

From meeting with and speaking to hundreds of thousands of parents and students for the past two decades, I have found one factor that has caused more student loans than anything else: PARENT GUILT. What is parent guilt? Picture this scenario: A college fair at the local high school gymnasium, packed with rows of college recruiters standing behind brightly colored tablecloths with pens, keychains and other cheap tchotchkes to be taken for free. Hundreds of high school juniors and seniors are excitedly buzzing from table to table, picking up brochures from colleges that are halfway across the country or private colleges that cost as much as $50,000/year. And trudging behind those students are scores of anxious parents, shoulders slumped, heads in their hands and distressed looks on their faces with one thought on their minds: "How in God's name are we going to afford this?" So here's what happened -- 17 years ago you had your little cherub, and in the back of your mind you knew this day would come. But you were busy being a good parent -- putting a roof over their head, clothes on their back and food on the table. And because you were busy being a good parent, you didn't take the time to start an Education Savings Account (ESA) or a 529 College Saving Plan. (Does any of that sound familiar?) And that's when the parent guilt washes over you. So when your little cherub -- now on the verge of adulthood -- looks at you all doe-eyed and asks you to spend $40,000 per year for their college tuition, you look at them and utter the 7 MOST DANGEROUS words any parent can say to their college-bound teen: "OK honey, whatever you want to do...." Those words turn into $100,000 in student loan debt and another $50,000 in Parent PLUS loans! And so begins the 30-year nightmare for parents and students alike.

I am here to RELEASE you from parent guilt. You have done a GREAT job as a parent. You have gotten your child this far -- they're alive, healthy and drug-free. Your job is to help get them through college, but BY NO MEANS should you feel any liability to let them go into massive student loan debt or let yourself go into parent debt to help pay for their education. DO NOT LET PARENT GUILT ruin your family's financial future.

Who runs your household: You or your child?

Now I have to get a little tough on the parents. As financial expert Dave Ramsey says, "We don't have a student loan crisis. We have a PARENTING crisis!" Millions of parents, plagued by the parent guilt we just discussed, are allowing their children to make horrible choices about where they go to college -- leading to massive debt loads and miserable lives. Parents, I'm BEGGING you to BE A PARENT! Ask yourself who runs your household: you or your 17-year-old? Are you going to allow your teen to dictate their choice of college? Are you going to allow them to make a decision that will harm their future for decades? We know how 17-year-olds think they know it all. I know I did at that age, and you parents reading this probably did, too -- and it's terrifying to contemplate *how little we actually knew* back then. And let's acknowledge that the 17-year-old human brain isn't fully developed. One might even call adolescence a form of brain damage -- LOL! The very serious bottom line here is these teens can hardly be expected to make such huge financial decisions or understand the implications and consequences of going $50K, $70K or $100K in debt for their college education. That is why I need you parents to step up and be a parent. DO NOT let your 17-year-old run your household! You've already been freed of your parent guilt, so be strong and decide that you're not going into debt or allowing your child to go into debt for their education. Make a decision based on the financial ability of your household, not on the whims and wishes of a teenager. You are the adults in the home, and they need you to act like it. Will they be mad, flop on the floor and foam at the mouth? Possibly. Just remember how at 4 years old they also threw a temper tantrum in the cereal aisle because you wouldn't buy the Sugary O's they wanted. As the parent, you decided it wasn't good for them, knowing the sugar would rot their teeth, and did what was best *for* them. Think of student loans as the Sugary O's of finance, then, since they will rot your family wallet for years to come. So once again, BE THE PARENT and do what is best for them and their future.

Why are Parent Loans a BAD idea?

We have spent the majority of our time addressing the drawbacks of student loans, but I want to make it extremely clear that parent loans are just as bad. Over the years I have seen countless examples of well-meaning folks taking out Parent PLUS loans to the tune of $50,000 -- and higher -- to help their children attend colleges they couldn't afford. What results are nightmare scenarios such as these:

1) One of the parents has a job loss and they can no longer make the payments

2) Parents fail to communicate their expectation for the child to pay back the loans, the child gets blindsided and the fallout leads to strained relations and even alienation

3) The child doesn't finish college and the parents are still on the hook for the massive loan and end up very resentful

This is a mere sampling of ugly situations I have witnessed. There are just too many things that can go wrong when you take out parent loans. Again, let go of your parent guilt and help your child choose a college that your family can afford based on your current financial situation and budget. There is a famous saying: "The road to hell is paved with good intentions." This is completely accurate when it comes to parent loans. Thinking they are doing a good thing for their child, millions of parents end up in financial hell trying to dig out of the hole they dug for themselves paying for their child's education. Do not risk your financial future -- and even your relationship with your child -- because you weren't strong enough to put your foot down and help them make a decision that is beneficial for everyone involved. Commit now: **NO PARENT PLUS LOANS FOR COLLEGE!**

Why are 401K loans for college an AWFUL idea?

I have seen many parents borrow against their retirement to pay for their child's college education. HUGE MISTAKE! DO NOT DO THIS! It's yet another example of parent guilt causing parents to make TERRIBLE choices to pay for college. Here is the reality: You've worked your entire life saving for your retirement -- which for most parents of college-bound teens is only about 15 to 20 years away. Do not sacrifice your life's savings to pay for a college that your family CANNOT afford! Here is the biggest reason why: 50% of students DO NOT GRADUATE - Well, there is a 100% chance that you are going to retire someday, while there is only a 50% chance that your child is going to graduate from college. So borrowing against or cashing out your retirement that you will 100% need in a few years to pay for something that only has a 50% chance of happening is a MASSIVE MISTAKE! Of course you THINK your child is going to graduate, but there are NO guarantees. So the worst-case scenario -- which has played out more times than you can imagine -- is the child has NO degree and the parent has NO retirement savings! That's a LOSE-LOSE for everyone involved.

The same goes for your home. DO NOT take out a second mortgage or a Home Equity Line of Credit (HELOC) to pay for college! DO NOT sacrifice your home or put it at risk for your child's education! If for some unforeseen reason you can't make the payments, you can lose your house. And what if your child doesn't graduate? Now you are homeless and your child has no degree. Trust me, IT HAPPENS! The worst mistake parents make is assuming that everything will work out fine and as planned. If you've been on this planet for more than 20 minutes, you know that life often DOES NOT work out as planned. And there is absolutely NO need to risk your home and livelihood trying to make up for the years that you weren't able to save for college. I will say it a thousand times: SEND YOUR CHILD TO THE COLLEGE YOUR FAMILY CAN AFFORD! And if you have take out ANY kind of debt to pay for it, here is the harsh reality: YOU CANNOT AFFORD IT!

You may not like my direct approach or my use of CAPITAL LETTERS to get my point across. But I am trying to YELL through these pages to keep you from making a mistake you and your family could regret for many years.

PLEASE be smart about how you pay for college; it's one of the most important choices you will ever make!

Why is Co-Signing a student loan the WORST idea?

O f all the poor choices that millions of parents make to pay for their child's education, hands down the WORST choice they make is to co-sign a student loan for their child. NEVER NEVER NEVER co-sign ANY kind of loan (car loan, house loan, etc) but ESPECIALLY do not co-sign a student loan. Just use common sense for a second. Why is a co-signer needed? Usually because the primary borrower doesn't have the credit history or financial history to qualify for the loan on their own. So the banks want a co-signer because they know there is a VERY good chance that the main borrower is NOT going to be able to re-pay the loan. So when they default on their payments (as they usually do), who does the bank go after? That's right - the CO-SIGNER! So if you co-sign for your child's student loans, there is about a 99% chance that YOU will end up re-paying the loan! I have seen more relationships ruined between parent and child over failure to pay co-signed student loans. The child is embarrassed they can't pay and end up avoiding the parent, and the parent is mad that their child didn't fulfill their financial obligation and they are left holding the bag. DO NOT DO THIS TO YOUR CHILD! Your relationship is far more valuable than money, so PLEASE do not let something like a student loan ruin your bond. Your child will end up not coming home for the holidays because they defaulted on their co-signed student loans! Is that really what you want?

Once again, no one ever considers the consequences of what can go wrong in these situations. They only look at the good side if everything works out perfectly. But as I already said, we know this is rarely the case. Don't let your good intentions destroy your relationship with your child. Your child is NOT going to re-pay the loan - it is GOING to fall on you - so again I am BEGGING you (I'm doing a lot of begging in this book) - DO NOT CO-SIGN YOUR CHILD'S STUDENT LOAN! It is one of the WORST mistakes you will ever make!

And if you need even more proof: Not to make this a religious conversation, but even the Bible says not to co-sign loans. Proverbs 17:18 says, "One who lacks sense gives a pledge and puts up security in the presence of his neighbor." So don't blame me - even God says it's STUPID to co-sign a loan! So even if you don't listen to me, listen to God - **NEVER CO-SIGN A STUDENT LOAN!**

What is the most important word parents have to learn?

There is a very important word that parents have to learn. Or I should say RE-learn. They used to say this word to their children all the time - several times a day in fact. But for some reason after 17 years of saying this word, when it comes to college, parents have forgotten this word. So let's re-learn this word together. It's very simple - you put your tongue to the roof of your mouth, make a kissing motion with your lips and it sounds like this - NO! Parents must learn to say NO to their high school seniors when it comes to going into debt for college. It sounds like this:

NO! I am not going to let you go 50, 70, or $100,000 in debt for a college you can't afford!

NO! I am not taking out a Parent PLUS loan to pay for your education!

NO! I am not going to borrow on or cash out my retirement or to pay for college!

NO! I am not going to take out a 2nd mortgage or a Home Equity Loan to pay for college!

NO! I am not going to co-sign for a student loan!

You might say this is tough love, but it's not. It's not tough love - it's LOVE. What is tough love when you kept your 4 year old from touching a hot stove? No. Was it tough love when you kept your 8 year old from running into the middle of traffic? No - it was love. Love is preventing your children from doing things that will cause them harm. The word NO kept them from physical harm, and now the word NO can keep them - and you - from financial harm.

These two little letters could actually end the student loan crisis in this country. If we had enough strong parents to re-learn this word, it would prevent billions of student loans and millions of ruined relationships every year. If enough strong parents re-learned this word, it could end the government student loan program and bring down insanely high tuition costs from colleges. I am on a mission to empower as many parents as possible to re-learn this word - as the title of the book says, Say YES to College - Say NO to College Debt!

Is it bad to go to an expensive college?

S ometimes when I speak to students, they will think I don't like expensive colleges or somehow think they are evil. I want to make something very clear. I have NO issue with expensive colleges. If you want to go to private colleges like Boston University, or Brandeis, or Babson - all colleges that cost upwards of $50,000 per year for tuition - that's completely fine. If you want to go across your state line and go to an out of state public college - which will cost you 3-4 times the price of staying close to home and going to an in-state public college - that's great. As long as you have the MONEY to attend the college, go wherever you want to go. If you win over $200,000 in college scholarships and you can afford whatever school you choose, go for it. If you parents have the money to write a check for $200,000 to pay for your education with no problem, awesome for you.

All I am saying and trying to convey to you is there is absolutely NO good reason to go into massive amounts of student loan debt, or have your parents go into debt to go to an expensive college. I made the analogy earlier - would you buy a $100,000 car you can't afford? Would you buy a $100,000 piece of jewelry you can't afford? Of course not. College is no different. Just like you won't get a return on that car or piece of jewelry, you won't get a return for going to THAT particular expensive college.

So while it's not bad to go to an expensive college in general, if you can't pay for it without debt, then it is VERY bad for you and your future.

How do I go to college debt free? (Pt. 1)

S o I hope I have given you enough reasons to understand why college debt is a terrible idea. So enough of dealing with the problem - let's talk solutions. How do you go to college and graduate DEBT FREE? Yes in today's world it can be done. There are 4 primary strategies to going to college with no debt.

The first main strategy to going to college is one we have talked about extensively already in this book - College Choice. College choice is the #1 factor in avoiding college debt and graduating debt free. You must choose the college your family can afford. Will it be your first choice of college? Maybe...maybe not. But there is nothing more important than graduating from college with a degree in your chosen field of study with ZERO debt. That one choice will set you up for long term success more than any other factor. So what are the colleges that give you best chance of avoiding college debt:

1. Community College. As I mentioned in an earlier chapter, community colleges are a great way to to start your education at a much lower cost. You can get your 2-year degree, and then transfer to a 4-year college. Or you may choose a career field where you only need a 2-year degree. Either way starting at a community college is an strategy to avoid debt, as the costs are very affordable. In fact, here in my home state of New Jersey, we have the NJ STARS program. If you graduate in the top 15% of your high school class, you can go to any community college in the state for FREE! That's F-R-E-E - the best 4-letter word in the dictionary! Look into any similar programs in your state.

2. In State Public Colleges. Again as discussed earlier in-state public colleges in most cases cost less than half (or even more) in tuition that in-state private colleges or out-of-state public colleges. You simply cannot justify paying 3 or 4 times more for the same college degree from 2 colleges. There is NO data that supports that a more expensive college gives a better education or gives a higher return on investment.

I will say it one more time if I haven't said it a hundred times already - CHOOSE THE COLLEGE YOUR FAMILY CAN AFFORD - that is the smartest way to attend college and the best way to graduate from college DEBT FREE!

How do I go to college debt free? (Pt. 2)

The next strategy to go to college debt free is one your students won't like: Commute from Home. Of course if you attend a community college, you really don't have a choice but to live at home. For the most part, community colleges don't offer on-campus housing. But for those of you attending in-state public 4 year colleges, commuting from home effectively cuts the cost of college in half. Room & board (as it is called by colleges) can usually cost up to another $15,000 per year. This covers housing and meal plans. So if you if choose to live at home you can save another $15,000 per year for college. Now of course, 99% of high school seniors are ready to fly the coop and get out of the house for the next 4 years at least, so many of them won't like this strategy. But remember what this book is about - it's not about having fun or having an awesome college experience by living in the dorm - it's about attending and graduating from college with ZERO DEBT. It's about smart CHOICES - choices that will set you up for long term success - not short term pleasure.

And once again - if you have the money to pay for on-campus housing, then pay for it. I'm simply saying don't take out student loans or parent loans just so your student can live in a dorm for 4 years. Remember what the goal is - Say NO to college debt. Does that involve tough choices? Yes. Does that involve doing things your student won't like? Yes. Trust me - a tougher choice is paying off $70,000 in student loans for the next 20 years. So if you make the tough choices now it will allow for easier choices in the future.

How do I go to college debt free? (Pt. 3)

The third strategy for going to college debt free is directed right to the students: Apply for 1000 scholarships. I'm serious - literally apply for 1000 scholarships. Getting scholarships for college is simply a numbers game - the more you apply for, the more you will receive. So make a plan to apply for as MANY scholarships as humanly possible. It doesn't matter how much the scholarship is for - $100, $200, $500 - every little bit helps and keeps your out of pocket costs down. When I attended Morgan State, most of my friends in my freshman year who couldn't come back sophomore year was not because of their grades - it was because they didn't have the money. Many parents can usually find a way to pay for the first year of college - it's years 2-4 that gets more difficult. So the more scholarships you apply for in high school, the less you will have to worry about in college how you are going to pay for it.

The best place to find scholarships to apply for is your guidance office. Your guidance counselor has access to TONS of scholarships that you can apply for, and are more than willing to help you. However, from working with thousands of counselors across the country, you know what I hear from them ALL the time: "Nash I can't get these seniors to apply for scholarships because they're lazy - they don't want to write the essays!" My best advice to you is write essay until your FINGERS fall off! Many times you can submit the same essay to apply for several scholarships - but whatever you have to do to apply - DON'T BE LAZY! Literally MILLIONS of dollars in scholarships go unclaimed by students every year simply because there was no one that applied for them - those are scholarships with YOUR name on it!

Another great source for scholarships are local organizations. They may be service organizations like Rotary or Lions Club, fraternities & sororities, or local businesses. Whatever they offer, apply for ANYTHING and EVERYTHING. As I mentioned in an earlier chapter your college applications should be submitted by Christmas of your senior year. This leaves your entire spring semester to focus on NOTHING but scholarship applications. Your entire part-time job should be applying for as many scholarships as possible. Think 5 a day - 25 a week - 100 per month. APPLY APPLY APPLY APPLY APPLY (Did I say APPLY?) for everything you can - even if you end up getting 30 out of 1000 - those 30 scholarships could completely pay for your college education. There are numerous stories of students who did just that - but it took LOTS of hard work - hard work that paid off tremendously for them. That student can be you!

And of course it goes without saying the best way to get scholarships is through your grades and test scores. Having the highest GPA possible puts you in a position to earn scholarships for college, so do your very best in the classroom. And as mentioned earlier taking a test prep course will help you get higher score on your SAT/ACT - which also is a huge factor for winning scholarships for college. I was very fortunate to earn a full academic scholarship to college, based on my grades and SAT scores. If you have taken your education seriously from your freshman year, you can be in position to do the same. Scholarships are the way to go!

How do I go to college debt free? (Pt. 4)

T he fourth and final strategy for going to college debt free will take work - and that's the strategy: WORK! A part-time job while in college is a great way to earn the money you need to help pay your way through school. No it is not child abuse for you to have a job in college - YOU CAN WORK! Even though I had a full academic scholarship to Morgan State, there are expenses that I had that weren't covered like laundry, snacks, phone cards (parents will have to explain to their child what a phone card is) So I worked part time at Taco Bell - that's right I was slingin' tacos and burrito supremes! It helped me earn enough extra money to pay for the things that my scholarship didn't pay for.

But even if you don't have a scholarship, working part-time can be the best way to pay for school. You can do things like deliver pizza at night or babysit. Some of you may even start your own business like cutting grass or building websites. Many colleges offer a work-study program - where you work part-time at the college (like in the dining hall or as an administrative assistant) The list is endless on what you can do to earn money for college.

So here's an example: Let's say you have a part-time job working 20 hours per week, getting paid $10/hour, and you work 50 weeks per year. Quick math: 20x10x50= $10,000 per year. That's sounds ALOT like an in-state tuition at a public college to me (if you commute from home). So please do not tell me that a student HAS to go $80,000 in debt to afford college - IT'S SIMPLY NOT TRUE! A student CHOOSES to go $80,000 in debt! They had less expensive options - they just chose the more expensive option that they couldn't afford. It's no different from car debt - You can CHOOSE to buy a $5,000 car for cash and have no car payments or you can CHOOSE to buy a $70,000 Range Rover that you can't afford and have payments of $700/month - It's a choice!

Not to mention the additional benefit of working in college - getting actual work experience. Research actually shows that students who work part-time in college actually have higher GPA's than students who don't work. Mainly because they have to manage their time more effectively - they don't have the time to hang out all night partying or playing beer pong. When they come from work, they actually study! And who do you think an employer is more likely to hire - a student who has actual work experience or a student with zero work experience? If a student can maintain grades and have a job at the same time, that student is VERY attractive to a potential employer after college.

So if you want to go to college debt free - **GO TO WORK!** It pays and it pays off!

What ONE book should EVERY family read about paying for college?

B esides this book (of course), there is ONE book that will help more families prepare for and pay for college than any other. In fact this ONE book, if read AND implemented, can do more to change the direction of your family's finances than any other. That book is: The Total Money Makeover by Dave Ramsey. If you've never heard of Dave Ramsey, he is someone you should get to know. He is the nationally syndicated host of The Dave Ramsey Show, the #3 ranked talk radio show in America. Every day he takes calls from listeners and advises them on their money issues, and teaches millions of people how to get out of debt and stay out of debt. He also teaches a video class called Financial Peace University, which is hosted in tens of thousands of churches throughout the United States. Dave Ramsey has done more to help people with their financial issues, and in the process created more wealthy people, than any other person on the planet - and he can help you too. You can learn more about him at www.daveramsey.com.

In The Total Money Makeover, you will learn what schools and American culture will NEVER teach you about money. Examples are:

- How to GET out of debt and STAY out of debt FOREVER

- Why you should NEVER get a credit card (Your points don't matter)

- Why you should NEVER have a car payment (Literally costing you millions)

- Why the credit score is a FALSE measure of financial success

- The right way to purchase a home and how to pay it off in 7-10 years

- How to save and invest for your retirement so you don't have to rely on Social Security or your children to take care of you

This is the ONE book I WISH I had read when I was 18 years old. I would have avoided SO many mistakes and would be SO much further along financially. I STRONGLY encourage you to pick up this book and READ IT with your family. I challenge you to read this book and go back to your old way of thinking about money and finances. There is old saying "Once the mind is stretched with idea or concept, it cannot go back to same way." That is a perfect way to describe The Total Money Makeover. In fact, I believe SO much in this book, I am making this offer: To ANY high school senior who reads this book and sends me a book summary (no less than 1000 words) on what you learned, I will send them a $100 gift card they can use to buy books in college. Send your summary to: nashspeaks@nashwarfield.com

READ THIS BOOK and get to know Dave Ramsey - **IT WILL CHANGE YOUR LIFE!!!**

CONCLUSION: What's next?

I started this book telling you that I am on a mission - a mission to educate families of high school students about the dangers of college debt. Hopefully after reading this book, you have helped me accomplish that mission. I hope that you believe that it is absolutely critical that you attend some form of higher education after high school. I hope that you have more information than when you started this book, and now understand that it is 100% POSSIBLE to attend and graduate from college DEBT FREE. I hope that you understand that the choices that you make today about paying for your education can either push you forward, or hold you back for the next 10, 20 or 40 years. I hope that you no longer believe the lies and myths that are pervasive in our culture about college, and you are now empowered to make smart choices about where you attend college and how you choose to pay for it. I have done all that I can to give you as much information as possible to turn the tide against this massive student loan crisis that we face in America today.

Now it's up to you. Will you take this book, put it on your shelf, and never touch it again? Will you disregard all that you have read, be a victim of parent guilt, and still decide to go into parent loan debt or let your child go into student loan debt? I learned about a year into speaking to students that I'm not responsible FOR them - I am only responsible TO them. I can only give the information - it's completely up to them what they will do with it. And so it is with you - I am not responsible for the decisions you make at this point about paying for college. But now you have the information. If 5 years from now you wake up with $100K in student loan debt, or $50K in parent loan debt, the one thing you cannot say "Nobody told me - I didn't know". Ignorance is no longer an excuse. Now it's about the choices that you make.

Will you join me on my mission? Will you take this info and not only use it for your own family, but share it with other families as well? One family at a time we can end the student loan crisis, bring down the insane rising cost of college, and help students to succeed both professionally and financially for many years to come. But I need your help - I can't do it alone. I encourage you to share this book with as many students and families as you know, and encourage them to do the same. I know it's cliche, but I believe we can do it

one family at a time - together. Together we can help millions of families to
SAY YES TO COLLEGE & SAY NO TO COLLEGE DEBT!!!

If you enjoyed this book, please give me a positive review on Amazon.
And if you have ANY questions about college, paying for college, or would
like me to speak at your high school, college or church, please email me at:
nashspeaks@nashwarfield.com

Additional Resources:

Getting INTO college:

You Got Into Where? (book) - Joi Wade (got admitted and won scholarships to top universities)

Paying for College:

www.myscholly.com (Scholarship website & app)

www.fastweb.com (Scholarship website)

The Ultimate Scholarship Book (New Edition annually)

Confessions of a Scholarship Winner (book) - Kristina Ellis (won over $500K in scholarships)

Other Books on Graduating Debt Free:

Debt Free U - Zac Bissonnette

Graduate with Zero Debt - Pallas Ziporyn

Zero Debt for College Grads - Lynnette Khalfani

Books on Succeeding In College:

Tricks of the Grade - Dr. Joe Martin

Making College Count (book) - Pat O'Brien (founded Making It Count Programs, a national speaking company that empowered millions of high school and college students from the early 2000s to 2010

Made in the USA
Lexington, KY
25 September 2018